Puberty & Periods

A Resource for Pre-Teen and Teenage Girls

EXTENDED EDITION

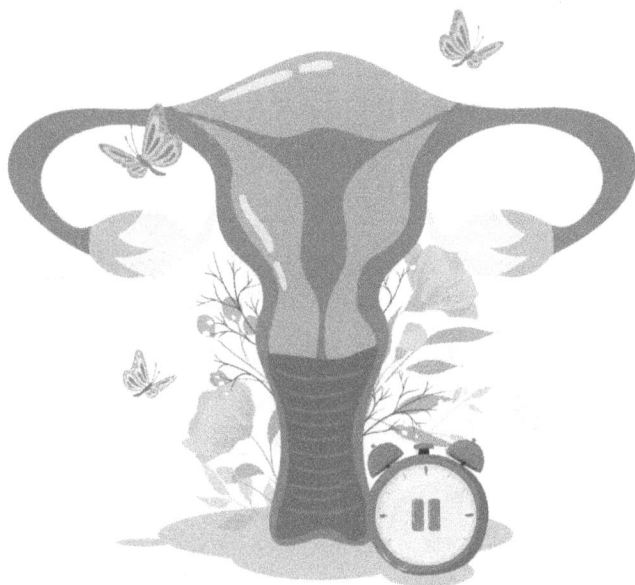

Written by Shantell Richards, Ed.S.

Illustrated by Mia Cleare

Contents

Contents

Growth & Change

Even before you exited your mother's womb (her uterus), your body was constantly developing. Once you entered the world, your physical body experienced more growth. Think about how much you've grown since infancy. Your body has undergone many changes in many different ways, including puberty. Puberty is also a natural change the body undergoes; however, it is considered a significant milestone in your development because it is when your reproductive organs develop. It also marks the time when girls can become pregnant. Changes brought on by puberty don't happen overnight; they are gradual… and can continue for two to five years. Some changes are subtle, such as mood swings or the growth of hair under your arms and on your genitalia. More obvious changes during puberty include widened hips, the development of your breasts, acne, and the start of your menstrual cycle.

Celebrating Puberty

"Menarche" is the official word to denote a girl's first period. While puberty can be seen as an unwanted and unwelcomed change for some girls, this stage of development is actually celebrated in some cultures. The "Sunrise Ceremony", which involves different rituals where girls from the tribe receive and offer gits – is a celebration that Native American tribes in North America host to pay tribute to girls reaching puberty. The ceremony signifies a girl's transition from childhood. In the Jewish faith girls between the ages of 12 and 13 participate in a celebration called a "bat mitzvah" to mark their transition from childhood.

Hormones

Hormones are like chemical messengers sent from the brain and different glands to be targeted areas of the body to achieve a specific goal.

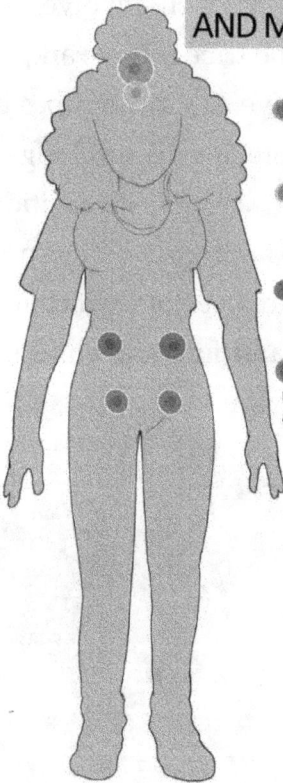

ENDOCRINE GLANDS AND MAJOR HORMONES

- **HYPOTHALAMUS**
  Governor of the Endocrine System
  Controls the pituitary gland

- **PITUITARY GLAND**
  Master Gland
  Secretes hormones that control other glands

- **ADRENAL GLANDS**
  Produces **testosterone** (in small amounts) that helps with sexual response

- **OVARIES**
  Produces **estrogen** that controls menstruation & **progesterone** that support pregnancy

Hormones are at the root of your body's further changes during puberty. They send messages to various parts of your body to grow. For example, particular hormones released from the pituitary gland target your ovaries and stimulate your ovaries to develop estrogen. The hormone estrogen is ultimately responsible for the different changes you may (or may not) notice during puberty; your body will experience a boost in estrogen production during this time. As you age, your body will produce less estrogen.

Other female hormones include estradiol, estrone, progesterone, testosterone, and androgens.

Mood Swings & Irritability

The hormones responsible for puberty are also responsible for the mood swings and irritability you may experience during puberty, especially during your period, because your hormones may fluctuate. It is essential to know that your mood may likely change during your period and that you may not feel so great emotionally. Knowing this helps you understand your emotions as they happen.

Suppose you're feeling grouchy or irritable during your periods. In that case, you can help yourself in the following ways -- make sure you're mindful of your diet. Avoiding unhealthy foods will also help you avoid random moodiness, irritability, and/or anxiety.

Also, exercising is vital during this time. Exercise can improve your mood because physical activity triggers and release "happy hormones" like dopamine and serotonin into your bloodstream. These hormones help you feel good. Give exercise a try! Finally, get into the habit of getting a minimum of seven hours of sleep each night. The amount of rest you obtain nightly directly affects your mood when you awaken; limited sleep means an increased likelihood of feeling tired, irritable, and grouchy.

Acne

Acne is another visible change that is often experienced by girls during puberty. Acne is caused by overactive oil glands beneath the skin; during puberty, oil glands get stimulated when hormones become active. A buildup of oil, dead skin cells and bacteria leads to inflammation (swelling and redness) in the pores – and that swelling shows up as a pimple. While acne is a common sign of puberty, not everyone experiences acne during it. Those who suffer from acne may only experience occurrences during puberty. However, acne is a problem faced by many adults as well. To avoid oil buildup and unwanted bacteria, wash your face two times a day with a gentle organic cleanser. Dead skin cells can be removed with exfoliants, such as organic sugar scrubs and skin masks.

Simple Organic Sugar Scrub Recipe

- 1 cup of cane organic sugar
- ½ cup of coconut oil or olive oil
- 5-7 drops of an essential oil that is known for its skin health benefits (optional)

To use your sugar scrub: lather the area where you want to apply the sugar scrub with a gentle soap, and then massage a small scoop of the sugar scrub into the area until the sugar scrub dissolves. Rinse with tepid water followed by a cool rinse.

Simple Organic Skin Mask Recipe

- 1 cup of organic honey (one of the best ingredients for a skin mask)
- ½ cup of apple cider vinegar (or lemon juice)

To use your skin mask: wash your face, apply mask and leave on skin for 20 minutes. Rinse with tepid water followed by a cool rinse.

Visible Body Hair

Social norms regarding women and body hair change depending on where you are in the world. More body hair can be expected during puberty. Hair can become more visible on the legs, armpits, and genitalia. In places like the United States, most women are expected to remove the hair from their legs, underarms, and genitalia. Women do this by shaving, waxing, using chemical hair removers, or using laser hair removal. In a country like China, however, most women do not engage in any practices to remove their body hair. Whether you decide to keep any of your body hair should be a personal choice you make.

Removing Body Hair

In cultures where body hair is seen as distasteful, shaving is usually the first experience a girl will have with removing hair from her legs, under her arms, and even her genitalia. The advantage of shaving is that it allows you to quickly remove unwanted hair however, there are also disadvantages to shaving that you should consider.

Hair that is shaved from an area tends to grow back quickly, and can grow back with a texture that is coarser. The blades on shavers can cause cuts if the shaver isn't used with caution, and shaving hair from an area can create discoloration (a change in the color of the skin) in that area. For example, you may notice that the skin under your arms has become darker after you start shaving. You will also likely experience itching in areas where you have shaved once hair begins to grow back.

Ingrown hairs are another problem associated with shaving. Ingrown hairs are unappealing, painful, and will likely itch. These bumps occur when hair starts to grow back and curves into the skin instead of growing out of the skin. Dead skin usually prevents the hair from growing out, so it curves inward and a "bump" forms. If the ingrown hair becomes infected the bump will grow and become more painful. This infection can lead to scarring on the skin.

The best way to prevent ingrown hairs is by exfoliating (removing dead skin cells) before shaving. You can use your organic sugar scrub recipe to exfoliate before shaving.

Growing Breasts

Enlarged breasts can also be expected during puberty. However, the amount of growth will vary for each girl. Some girls will develop large breasts, while others will develop small ones. There are even instances where a girl goes through puberty but doesn't grow any breasts. Breast size is measured in "cups," and knowing your cup size helps you purchase a properly fitting bra. Bra/cup sizes range from A1 (smallest) to DD5 (largest). Girls who develop large breasts need bras that offer the proper support because having large breasts can create lots of back pain. The pain can sometimes require breast reduction surgery, where a

13

surgeon performs an operation to make the breasts much smaller.

Properly Measuring Your Breast Size

There are some girls who are blessed to belong to families filled with women, and it's in families like those that the older women can simply look at a girl and determine the proper bra size to fit her. For other girls, to get a bra that truly fits them properly they would need to have their measurements taken, because there are math calculations involved in determining correct bra size.

In addition to providing your breasts with support, a bra should be comfortable – and when you aren't wearing the correct size bra (too small or too large) you miss out on that support and comfortability.

Ovulation

Ovulation is one of the invisible changes that occurs once puberty starts in girls and occurs every month, approximately twelve to fourteen days before the start of your period. This process involves your reproductive organs and is directly tied to your monthly periods. Ovulation is also directly tied to your ability to have babies. When your body is ovulating, a mature egg is released from your ovary. After the egg is released, it moves down your fallopian tube and stays there for twelve to twenty-four hours, where it can be fertilized. If the egg is fertilized, a baby will develop inside the uterus. If the egg does not become fertilized, the lining of the uterus (called the endometrium) is shed. This shedding is what we call a menstrual cycle.

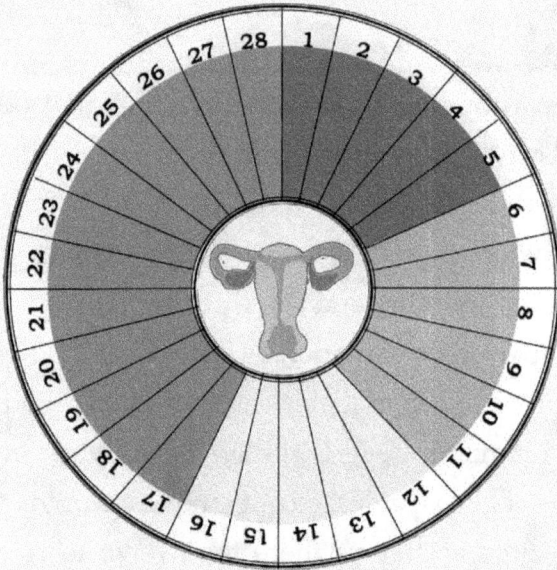

● PERIOD PHASE

● FOLLICULAR PHASE

● FERTILE WINDOW

● LUTEAL PHASE

The Onset of the Menstrual Cycle

"Menstrual cycle," "cycle," "menses," "period," and "moon cycle" are all terms that refer to the time of the month when your blood flow begins. Nicknames you may also hear that refer to the menstrual cycle include "a visit from Aunt Flo," "a visit from Mother Nature," and "that time of the month."

Ever wonder why the word "cycle" is included with words associated with a period? It's because a cycle refers to a repeating pattern, and normal or "regular" periods follow a repeating pattern. For some girls, their menstrual cycle begins every twenty-eight days;

for others, it may start every twenty-five days, every twenty-one days, etc. Keep track of your periods so that you know the pattern of your own menstrual cycle. Knowing this pattern allows you to determine exactly when your period will begin each month. This predictability allows you to be ready and prepared for each monthly menstrual cycle.

You can use monthly calendars or a menstrual tracking app to help you keep track of your periods. Most tracking apps will tell you when to expect your next period. If you're using a calendar, count how many days have passed from the start of your last period to the beginning of your next new period. You can do this three or four times, in different (consecutive) months. Each time you count, the total number of days from the start of one period to the start of the next new period should be the same. If/when a menstrual cycle doesn't follow a specific pattern, the periods are referred to as "irregular periods."

Discharge
and Pantyliners

The white discharge you may see before your before is called "leukorrhea" – and is filled with fluid and cells that are being shed from the vagina. This discharge may even look yellow at times. This part of your menstrual cycle is associated with the "luteal" phase, a time when the hormone progesterone peaks in your body.

Shifts in hormone levels can cause you experience a change in vaginal discharge. This is usually considered normal however sometimes discharge is a sign of an unhealthy vaginal environment and can be an indicator of infection.

Pantyliners, which are much smaller and thinner than the sanitary napkins used for period flow management, can be used for discharge management during the luteal phase of your menstrual cycle. If you are experiencing heavy discharge, discolored discharge, and/or odorous discharge it is likely you have some form of a vaginal infection and will need to be seen by a medical professional.

Menstrual Disorders

Oligomenorrhea is the official term for irregular periods. An irregular period is just one of many menstrual disorders. While this disorder may not cause pain, it causes anxiety because those suffering from it have unpredictable periods. Their periods can begin at unexpected times, on unexpected days, leaving them in a panic to quickly protect themselves from bleeding through their clothing.

Nearly all women will suffer from one or more menstrual disorders in their lifetime. While some menstrual disorders occur during adulthood, other menstrual disorders also affect pre-teens and teenagers. Diet and lifestyle habits are directly related to the development of some menstrual disorders.

Types of
Menstrual Disorders

Premenstrual Syndrome (PMS)

PMS is the term used to describe the physical and emotional changes that occur approximately a week before the start of a menstrual cycle. Common symptoms include bloating, moodiness, sadness, irrita-bility, anxiety, and anger.

Premenstrual Dysphoric Disorder (PMDD)

PMDD is a condition similar to PMS, but PMDD symptoms are heightened, and mood swings are incredibly intense. PMS is far more common than PMDD.

Premenstrual Exacerbation

Premenstrual exacerbation is a disorder where the mood swings caused by hormonal PMS act as an accelerant on pre-existing depression, anxiety, or bipolar disorder in a woman.

Dysmenorrhea

Dysmenorrhea is the term used to describe painful periods (including menstrual cramps, headaches, body aches, and pain); this is the most common menstrual disorder. Using over-the-counter pain medication (pain pills) to deal with menstrual pain has become normalized for women. However, extended use over long periods can potentially cause severe liver damage.

Amenorrhea

Amenorrhea is a menstrual disorder characterized by the absence of a menstrual cycle. Amenorrhea can sometimes occur after childbirth, although longer-lasting cases are most likely to happen when hormonal birth control has been taken over an extended period. Often, even once birth control is discontinued, it can take years for the menstrual cycle to begin again.

Menorrhagia

Menorrhagia is a menstrual disorder characterized by heavy or prolonged bleeding. It could be the most dangerous menstrual disorder of all.

Treatment for Menstrual Disorders

Hormones can be used to treat menstrual disorders in a variety of ways. Some hormones can help control heavy bleeding, while other hormones can stop ovaries from releasing eggs (which prevents a menstrual cycle from taking place). For pain associated with menstruation, over-the-counter medications like ibuprofen are recommended. Be mindful to never use aspirin for pain management during your period because it can cause heavier bleeding. Loss of large amounts of blood can lead to serious health issues, including death.

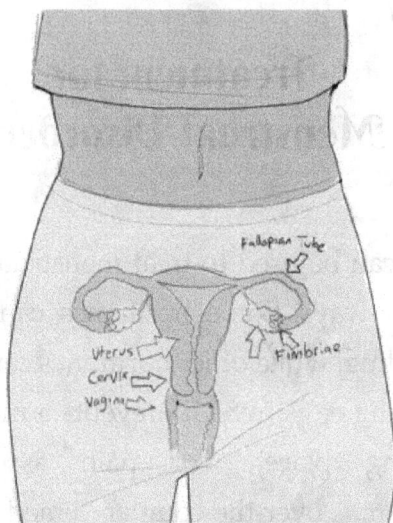

Female Reproductive Disorders

Diet plays a role in the development of certain reproductive disorders. A disorder is an abnormality in the
body that prevents the body from working properly.
Female reproductive disorders affect a woman's
monthly menstrual cycle and/or a woman's ability to
have a baby. Often, the causes of these disorders are
unknown – and treatment will usually involve surgery.

Endometriosis

Endometriosis is often a painful disorder where tissue similar to the tissue that usually lines the inside of your uterus — the endometrium — grows outside your uterus. Endometriosis most commonly involves your ovaries, fallopian tubes, and the tissue lining your pelvis. Rarely, endometrial-like tissue may be found beyond the area where pelvic organs are located.

With endometriosis, the endometrial-like tissue acts as endometrial tissue would — it thickens, breaks down, and bleeds with each menstrual cycle. But because this tissue cannot exit your body, it becomes trapped. When endometriosis involves the ovaries, cysts called endometriomas may form. Surrounding tissue can become irritated, eventually developing scar tissue and adhesions, which are bands of fibrous tissue that can cause pelvic tissues and organs to stick together.

Endometriosis can cause pain — sometimes severe — especially during menstrual periods. Fertility problems also may develop. Fortunately, effective treatments are available. The primary symptom of endometriosis is pelvic pain, often associated with menstrual periods. Although many experiences cramping during their menstrual periods, those with endometriosis typically describe menstrual pain far worse than usual. Pain also may increase.

Uterine Fibroids

Uterine fibroids are noncancerous growths of the uterus that often appear during the childbearing years. Also called leiomyomas or myomas, uterine fibroids aren't associated with an increased risk of uterine cancer and rarely develop into cancer. Fibroids range in size from seedlings undetectable by the human eye to bulky masses that can distort and enlarge the uterus. You can have a single fibroid or multiple ones. In extreme cases, multiple fibroids can expand the uterus so much that it reaches the rib cage and can add weight.

Many women have uterine fibroids during their lives. However, you might not know you have uterine fibroids because they often cause no symptoms. Your doctor may discover fibroids incidentally during a pelvic exam or prenatal ultrasound. Many women who have fibroids don't have any symptoms. Symptoms can be influenced by the location, size, and number of fibroids in those that do.

PCOS

Polycystic Ovary Syndrome (PCOS) is a problem with hormones during the reproductive years. If you have PCOS, you may not have periods very often. Or you may have periods that last many days. You may also have too much of a hormone called androgen in your body.

With PCOS, many tiny sacs of fluid develop along the outer edge of the ovary called cysts. The small fluid-filled cysts contain immature eggs. These are called follicles. The follicles fail to regularly release eggs.

The exact cause of PCOS is unknown. Early diagnosis and treatment and weight loss may lower the risk of long-term complications such as Type 2 Diabetes and heart disease. Symptoms of PCOS often start around the time of the first menstrual period. Sometimes symptoms develop later after you have had periods for a while.

Tubal Blockage

Fallopian tubes are female reproductive organs that connect the ovaries and the uterus. Every month during ovulation, which occurs roughly in the middle of a menstrual cycle, the fallopian tubes carry an egg from an ovary to the uterus. Conception also happens in the fallopian tube. If an egg is fertilized by sperm, it moves through the tube to the uterus for implantation. If a fallopian tube is blocked, the passage for sperm to get to the eggs and the path back to the uterus for the fertilized egg is blocked. Common reasons for blocked fallopian tubes include scar tissue, infection, and pelvic adhesions.

Blocked fallopian tubes don't often cause symptoms. Many women don't know they have blocked tubes until they try to get pregnant and have trouble. Sometimes, blocked fallopian tubes can lead to mild, regular pain on one side of the abdomen. This usually happens in a type of blockage called a hydrosalpinx. This is when fluid fills and enlarges a blocked fallopian tube.

Conditions leading to a blocked fallopian tube can cause their own symptoms. For example, endometriosis often causes painful periods and pelvic pain. It can increase your risk of blocked fallopian tubes. Blocked fallopian tubes are a common cause of infertility. Sperm and an egg meet in the fallopian tube for fertilization. A blocked tube can prevent them from joining.

Premature Ovarian Insufficiency

Premature ovarian insufficiency is a condition that occurs in women under the age of 40 whose ovaries do not function normally. Since the ovaries do not function as they should, the menstrual cycle stops prior to menopause.

Some reproductive disorders – like fibroids – can be treated medically/surgically. While other disorders, like endometriosis, are usually treated with hormones that will suspend the menstrual cycle. In severe cases surgery may be necessary to remove excess endometrial tissue that is growing outside of the uterus. "Endometrial ablation", which is only used when other therapies for endometriosis have failed, is a final option; during this procedure the lining of the uterus is destroyed.

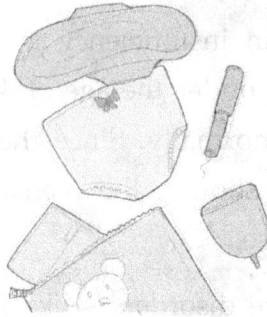

The Evolution of Sanitary Products

The range of commercial sanitary products available for period flow management has evolved over the past few decades. We now have more options than ever before!

Sanitary Napkins

Sanitary napkins, frequently referred to as "pads," are the most commonly used item (globally) for period flow management. These pads are placed directly inside your underwear to absorb menstrual flow. They usually contain an adhesive strip to keep them in place. When using sanitary napkins for period flow management, they should be changed (duration).

The idea for sanitary napkins was inspired by war bandages used on soldiers by French nurses. The first sanitary napkins were made available for purchase in 1888 – and since that time, the design of the sanitary napkin has undergone several changes so that they are less bulky, more absorbent, and more comfortable. The downside to sanitary napkins is that most brands are created using cotton grown with toxic pesticides and then bleached with chlorine to give products their pure white color. The pesticides and chlorine in these products should be nowhere near a vagina! To avoid these harmful toxins, organic sanitary napkins should be considered.

Tampons

Tampons, usually made of cotton, are temporarily inserted into the vagina to absorb menstrual flow. When using tampons for period flow management, they should be changed every couple of hours or as the flow dictates.

The idea of using tampons for period management is not new. The women in ancient Rome created items very similar to tampons using wool; ancient Indonesian women used vegetable fibers, African women used grass, and Japanese women used paper. The modern-day tampon was first introduced in 1931 and expanded women's options for period flow management. The use of tampons became a preferred method for many women because they allow them to be more physically active while menstruating.

The most significant downside to using tampons is the potential for experiencing toxic shock syndrome (TSS). TSS is a rare, life-threatening bacterial infection. Also, like sanitary napkins, tampons are typically made with cotton containing pesticides and bleached using chlorine. To avoid these harmful toxins, organic tampons can be used instead.

Inserting tampons may be difficult for virgins to achieve. Some parents do not allow their pre-teen and teenage daughters to wear tampons because the product has to be inserted into the vagina, so always talk to your parents before experimenting with tampons.

Period Panties

Period panties, also called "period-proof panties," are among the newest concepts for period flow management. The act of wearing/using period panties is called "free bleeding." Period panties look like regular underwear; however, they're designed to absorb menstrual flow. These panties are created using a moisture-wicking fabric that traps menstrual flow and keeps it from leaking onto clothing. When using period panties for menstrual flow management, panties should be changed and cleaned at least every twelve hours (or more often if needed).

The downside to using period panties is that you feel your menstrual flow, which may be quite unsettling if you're accustomed to using traditional sanitary items like pads and tampons. You may believe that your menstrual blood is leaking onto and staining your clothes (because you feel the flow) even though that isn't happening.

Menstrual Cups and Discs

Menstrual cups and menstrual discs are also reasonably new items now available to women for period flow management. Both cups and discs collect blood by being inserted into the vagina and can be worn for up to twelve hours. These items are not ideal for virgins since insertion may be difficult.

Menstrual cups and discs help women overcome many limitations and problems associated with using traditional items like sanitary napkins and tampons. Women who opt for this form of period flow management prefer using the menstrual cup over menstrual discs because cups are sturdier, easier to insert/remove and create less mess.

While a menstrual disc is disposable and can be flushed, a menstrual cup is reusable and requires sterilization before re-insertion. The downside to using menstrual cups and discs is that they are both messy to a certain degree, since there is a strong possibility of coming into contact with stored blood during removal. Using a menstrual cup that isn't cleaned correctly can cause infection.

Hygiene and Sanitation Habits

Your menstrual cycle might be the most significant change that puberty brings your way. Once your period begins, you must be more mindful of your restroom habits, especially since having a period means dealing with blood (which can be messy and smelly).

Developing the hygiene and sanitation habits listed below will allow you to maintain a high level of self-respect and respect for others during your periods.

Healthy Hygiene Habits

Healthy hygiene habits ensure you remain clean and odor-free during your period.

1. Avoid wearing sanitary napkins for an extended period. Doing so increases the likelihood of oxygen mixing with the napkin's blood, creating an unpleasant odor.
2. Always wash your hands before changing pads, tampons, or sanitary products. You never want

to touch your genitalia with unclean hands/ fingers.

3. Use an organic feminine cleansing spray or wipes to cleanse the genitalia and anal areas after removing sanitary napkins, tampons, menstrual cups, or menstrual discs. Properly cleaning these areas ensures that old blood and any pathogens from fecal matter (poop) are removed from the skin before a new sanitary item is used. This also helps to prevent any unwanted odors.

4. Wash hands immediately after changing sanitary napkins, tampons, etc. This ensures no blood is on your hands or fingers upon exiting the restroom.

Healthy Sanitation Habits

Healthy sanitation habits ensure that you properly dispose of sanitary products once they have been used. This shows self-respect and respect to everyone else you have to share a restroom with (public restrooms included).

1. When using sanitary napkins, completely wrap the used pad in tissue paper before placing it in

a trash can/bin. Once wrapped in tissue, no blood from the pad should be visible, and none of the sanitary napkin should be visible.

2. Never flush sanitary napkins! This will clog a toilet and prevent it from flushing properly.

3. Used tampons should be flushed immediately upon removal. No blood or any part of the used tampon should be exposed inside a trash bin. Do not place in a trash bin unless the tampon is fully wrapped in tissue paper.

4. Avoiding flushing tampons alongside large amounts of tissue, as this may also cause clogging, preventing a toilet from flushing properly.

Glossary of Terms

- **Adrenal glands**: Adrenal glands are glands that produce a variety of hormones.

- **Amenorrhea**: Amenorrhea is the absence of menstruation, often defined as missing one or more menstrual periods. Primary amenorrhea refers to the absence of menstruation in someone who has not had a period by age fifteen.

- **Bat mitzvah**: A bat mitzvah is a "coming of age" ritual for girls in Judaism.

- **Discharge**: Discharge is a mix of fluid and cells from the vagina.

- **Dopamine**: Dopamine is a type of neurotransmitter and hormone. It plays a role in many important body functions, including movement, memory, and pleasurable reward and motivation. High or low dopamine levels are associated with several mental health and neurological diseases.

- **Dysmenorrhea**: Dysmenorrhea is the medical term for painful menstrual periods caused by uterine contractions. Primary dysmenorrhea refers to recurrent pain, while secondary dysmenorrhea results from reproductive system disorders.

- **Egg**: The egg cell, or ovum, is the female reproducetive cell, or gamete.

- Endometrial ablation: a surgery that destroys the lining of the uterus

- **Endometrium**: The endometrium is the uterus's inner epithelial layer, along with its mucous membrane.

- **Estrogen**: Estrogen is a category of sex hormone responsible for the development and regulation of the female reproductive system and secondary sex characteristics.

- **Exfoliate**: Exfoliating is the process of removing dead skin cells and built-up dirt from the skin's surface.

- **Fallopian tubes**: The fallopian tubes are bilateral conduits between the ovaries and the uterus in the female pelvis. They function as channels for oocyte transport and fertilization.

- **Fecal matter**: Fecal matter is the solid or semi-solid remains of food not digested in the small intestine and broken down by bacteria in the large intestine.

- **Follicular phase**: The follicular phase is the part of the menstrual cycle when an egg matures in the ovaries.

- **Genitalia**: The male or female reproductive organs. The genitalia includes internal and external structures. The female internal genitalia are the ovaries, fallopian tubes, uterus, cervix, and vagina. The female external genitalia are the labia minora and majora (the vulva) and the clitoris.

- **Hormones**: A hormone is a class of signaling molecules in multicellular organisms sent to distant organs by complex biological processes to regulate physiology and behavior.

- **Hygiene**: Personal hygiene refers to maintaining the body's cleanliness.

- **Hypothalamus**: The hypothalamus is a part of the brain that coordinates the activity of the pituitary gland.

- **Inflammation**: Inflammation is part of the body's defense mechanism. It is the process by which the immune system recognizes and removes harmful and foreign stimuli and begins the healing process. Inflammation can be acute or chronic.

- **Ingrown hairs**: An ingrown hair is a hair that curves into the skin (instead of out of the skin) as it begins to grow.
- **Irregular period**: An irregular period is when the length of your menstrual cycle unexpectedly falls outside of your regular range. Irregular periods can include abnormal uterine bleeding, such as bleeding or spotting between periods, bleeding after sexual intercourse, heavy bleeding during your period, menstrual bleeding that lasts longer than normal, or bleeding after you've reached menopause.
- **Leukorrhea**: Leukorrhea is the medical term for vaginal discharge; this kind of discharge is mild, odorless, clear or milky in color – and is the natural byproduct of a healthy vagina
- **Luteal phase**: The luteal phase is the second part of the menstrual cycle, which prepares the uterus for pregnancy by thickening the uterine lining.
- **Menarche**: Menarche is the official term for the first occurrence of menstruation.
- **Menorrhagia**: Menorrhagia is the medical term for menstrual periods with abnormally heavy or prolonged bleeding.

- **Menstrual cup**: A menstrual cup is a type of reusable feminine hygiene product. It's a small, flexible funnel-shaped cup made of rubber or silicone that you insert into your vagina to catch and collect period fluid.

- **Menstrual cycle**: The menstrual cycle is the monthly series of changes a woman's body goes through to prepare for the possibility of pregnancy. Hormonal changes prepare the uterus for pregnancy. Each month, one ovary releases an egg — a process called ovulation. If ovulation takes place and the egg isn't fertilized, the lining of the uterus sheds through the vagina. This is a menstrual period.

- **Menstrual disc**: A menstrual disc is a flat, flexible disc that collects blood during your period rather than absorbing it, as pads, tampons, or period underwear do. The disc sits just below your cervix in your vaginal fornix.

- **Menstrual disorder**: Menstrual disorders are problems that affect a woman's normal menstrual cycle. They include painful cramps during menstruation, abnormally heavy bleeding, or not having any bleeding.

- **Ovaries**: The ovaries are small, oval-shaped glands on either side of your uterus. They produce and store your eggs (also called an ovum) and make hormones that control your menstrual cycle and pregnancy.

- **Ovulation**: Ovulation is the process in which a mature egg is released from the ovary. After it's released, the egg moves down the fallopian tube and stays there for 12 to 24 hours, where it can be fertilized.

- **Pantyliners**: a pantyliner is a thin, absorbent material placed inside of underwear to provide a layer of protection against discharge or light menstrual flow.

- **Pathogen**: A pathogen is defined as a disease-causing organism.

- **Period flow management**: Period flow management refers to the practices/products related to safely collecting fluid during a menstrual cycle.

- **Period panties**: Period panties or menstrual panties are designed with super absorbent materials to absorb the period flow. These panties replace pads and tampons.

- **Pituitary gland**: The Pituitary gland, also known as the hypophysis, is a pea-sized endocrine gland at the base of our brain. It is often referred to as the 'Master Gland' because it produces some of the important hormones in the body.

- **PMDD:** Premenstrual dysphoric disorder (PMDD) is a more serious form of premenstrual syndrome (PMS). PMS causes bloating, headaches, and breast tenderness a week or two before your period.

- **PMS**: Premenstrual syndrome (PMS) refers to emotional and physical symptoms that regularly occur in the one to two weeks before the start of each menstrual period. Symptoms resolve around the time menstrual bleeding begins.

- **Premature ovarian insufficiency**: Premature ovarian insufficiency is a loss of the normal function of the ovaries before age 40

- **Premenstrual exacerbation**: Premenstrual Exacerbation refers to the premenstrual exacerbation/ worsening of the symptoms of another disorder, such as major depressive disorder or generalized anxiety disorder.

- **Progesterone**: Progesterone is a hormone released in the ovary that plays a core role in the menstrual cycle and in maintaining the early stages of pregnancy.

- **Puberty:** Puberty is the process of physical changes through which a child's body matures into an adult body capable of sexual reproduction. It is initiated by hormonal signals from the brain to the ovaries in a girl.

- **Reproductive disorder**: A reproductive disorder is any condition that affects the normal function of the reproductive system, which can lead to issues with fertility.

- **Reproductive organs**: The female reproductive organs are the vagina, womb (uterus), fallopian tubes, and ovaries.

- **Sanitary napkin**: A sanitary napkin is a pad of absorbent material, such as cotton, worn by women during menstruation to absorb the uterine flow.

- **Sanitation:** Sanitation refers to proper disposal of human waste and the prevention of human contact with waste.

- **Serotonin**: Serotonin is a chemical that carries messages between nerve cells in the brain and throughout your body. Serotonin plays a key role in body functions, such as mood, sleep, digestion, nausea, wound healing, bone health, blood clotting, and sexual desire.

- **Social norms**: Social norms are shared standards of acceptable behavior by groups. Social norms can both be informal understandings that govern the behavior of members of society and be codified into rules and laws.

- **Sunrise ceremony**: A sunrise ceremony is the celebration of the beginning of the menstrual cycle for Native American girls living in North America.

- **Tampon**: A tampon is a menstrual product designed to absorb blood and vaginal secretions by insertion into the vagina during menstruation. Unlike a pad, it is placed internally inside the vaginal canal. Once inserted correctly, a tampon is held in place by the vagina and expands as it soaks up menstrual blood.

- **Uterus:** The uterus is a hollow muscular organ in the female pelvis between the bladder and rectum. The ovaries produce eggs that travel through the fallopian tubes. Once the egg has left the ovary, it can be fertilized and implanted in the uterus lining.

- **Vaginal infection**: A vaginal infection occurs whenever bacteria, fungus or a virus is introduced into the vaginal environment – which may subsequently result in abnormal discharge, odor, itching, irritation, and inflammation
- **Virgin**: Virgin is a person who has not had sexual intercourse.

About the Author

The author is a native of Miami, Florida and earned a Sociology degree from Rollins College in 2000. After working as an educator for 13 years the author founded 4EverFresh Feminine Care Products, which is now a global care and hygiene brand. In an effort to assist young girls, especially high-performing girls living in high-risk environments, the author also founded 4EverFresh Girls, Inc – a 501(c)3 nonprofit organization that serves girls throughout the United States. Empowerment through education lies at the center of the 4EverFresh brand, and so Puberty & Periods was created to teach young girls about their bodies and safe ways to care for their bodies.